MW01240574

POWER CHARGE Your Mind

40-Day Empowerment Journal

Affirm the Mind by Speaking Life

———————————

Caris L. Reed

Power Charge Your Mind 40-Day Empowerment Journal: Affirm the Mind by Speaking Life

ISBN-10: 198-36-86190
ISBN-13: 978-1983686191

Dedication

The *Power Charge* Your Mind 40-Day Empowerment Journal is dedicated to you, I personally want to give you this opportunity to enjoy a new path of a continuous positive mindset. A life you deserve free from drama, negativity, and complaining. Read each positive affirmation page, speak life, and write your heart out. Focus your mind on positive thoughts, relax and enjoy!

Thank You Page

I would like to thank everyone who tried to ruin my days with negative outbursts. You tried to get me out of character, yet some even succeeded. Just know you only motivated me to be the change in my own life.

I thank Caris, yes myself for no longer responding to negative people, issues, or thoughts. I no longer chose to walk or think in defeat. But rather I speak life into my circumstances.

I thank my mother for all the positive reinforcement you would give me when I was discouraged. Thank you for the laughter to lift my spirits.

Declaration

I declare that the defeat of doubt or negativity is no longer my portion. I walk in a sound mind given to me freely from the Lord. I am in control of my thoughts, words, and the actions that are behind them. I chose to speak life in all areas of my whole self to fulfil my God given purpose and destiny.

"I am in control of my thoughts; my thoughts are not in control of Me"

Introduction

Often, we can be our own worse critics, we tell ourselves we are not pretty or handsome, we can't do this or that. We say we are not as good as this person, if I just had a body like him or her. My nose is too big or to small, my this my that. We devalue and degrade our God-given beauty and talents because we refuse to put ourselves to a new standard, a new level, a new mindset.

I want you to begin a new journey for your life as you write in this journal. I need you to charge your mind on the scriptures in the book. Write them down before you write anything else on the pages. I need you to make yourself the star of this Empowerment journal. I believe at the end of this forty-day journal you will have the desire to rethink, retrain, and redevelop your thoughts of "you". Now is the time to rise and charge your mind

You must grow to oversee your mind and thoughts. For some it will be easy and for others they need a guide. Our minds are a masterpiece created by the highest God. It requires you to invest in developing it to the stature of His standards. The Lord tells us "Do not be conformed to this world, but be ye transformed the renewing of your mind" (Rom. 12:2).

In charging our minds it will require you to dig deep in your time and committing to this journal. It will require you to learn some new thoughts. The enemy wishes to have you believe it is hard to transform your mind from negative to positive, from doubt to belief, and from wishing to fruition. But right now, I speak life into you no longer will you be fearful of journalizing your worth, your positive thoughts, or your God-given visions.

This will take strong courage for you to speak to your mind. You need to believe with your whole heart, and use faith to control your thinking. In the next 40-days you will shift your thinking. You will become bolder in declaring change while using the power of tongue to charge your mind. In doing so you must believe that what you speak is done. Each day as you write in this life-changing journal prepare your mind for next level thinking. Speak the word over your life and practice scripture daily in your mind. I'm excited to be a part of this journey with you as we agree for your happiness, new thoughts, new level, and new positive mindset. Happy Journaling!

Section One

Power of Speaking Life

Inspiration

"Death and Life are in the power of the tongue, And those who love it will eat its fruit" (Proverbs 18:21) NKJV

Thought to ponder:

Our lives largely reflect the fruit of our tongue, to speak life is to speak God's perspective on any issue of your life; to speak death is to declare life's negative, to declare defeat, or complain constantly. As you begin this forty-day journal you must speak positive life in every situation. Whatever is bad or negative speak the opposite and believe things will turn around. After you written on these pages begin to speak it. Now believe with your faith and repeat if necessary daily creating an atmosphere and presence of the Lord and peace.

"Your will make your prayer to Him, And He will hear your vows. You will also declare a thing, And, it shall be established for you; So, light will shine on your ways" (Job. 22:27-28). NKJV

Day One

"Life is about getting better every day"

Day Two

"Make your mind work for you, not against you"

Day Three

"Decide, Commit, Succeed"

_____

_____

_____

_____

_____

_____

_____

_____

_____

_____

_____

_____

_____

_____

_____

_____

_____

_____

_____

_____

_____

Day Four

"You have the power to do anything with the right mindset"

Day Five

"Train your mind to see the good in every situation"

_____

_____

_____

_____

_____

_____

_____

_____

_____

_____

_____

_____

_____

_____

_____

_____

_____

Day Six

"Write down things you want to improve"

_____

_____

_____

_____

_____

_____

_____

_____

_____

_____

_____

_____

_____

_____

_____

_____

_____

_____

_____

_____

_____

_____

_____

_____

_____

_____

_____

_____

_____

_____

_____

_____

_____

_____

_____

_____

_____

_____

_____

_____

_____

_____

_____

_____

Day Seven

"Nothing worth having comes easy"

Day Eight

"Desire to change, must be greater than desire to remain"

_____

_____

_____

_____

_____

_____

_____

_____

_____

_____

_____

_____

_____

_____

_____

_____

_____

_____

_____

_____

_____

Day Nine

"Better thoughts, Better decisions, Better actions"

_____

_____

_____

_____

_____

_____

_____

_____

_____

_____

_____

_____

_____

_____

_____

_____

_____

_____

_____

Day Ten

"Refuse to entertain negativity"

_____

_____

_____

_____

_____

_____

_____

_____

_____

_____

_____

_____

_____

_____

_____

_____

_____

_____

_____

_____

Day Eleven

"Believe you were born to achieve greatness"

Day Twelve

"Be to positive for doubt"

Day Thirteen

"Let positive energy be your language"

Section Two

Power of Vision

Inspiration

"Write the vision and make it plain on tablets, that he may run who

reads it. For the vision is for an appointed time; But at the end it will

speak, and not lie, though it tarries, wait for it; Because it will surely

come, it will not tarry"

(Hab. 2:2-3). NKJV

Thought to ponder:

Journalize things the Lord speaks to you or quickens to your heart. Mediate on Bible promises and believe what He says will come to pass. Whatever vision God give you make it plain and run with it. When the time is right use resources to bring it to pass.

Use this section to not only speak life in your circumstances through your writing but, journalize any business visions whether big or small. List goals and plans for your life or business and after you write them speak them in the atmosphere as you pray for the blessings of God upon them.

Day Fourteen

"Be proud of your progress"

_____

_____

_____

_____

_____

_____

_____

_____

_____

_____

_____

_____

_____

_____

_____

_____

_____

_____

_____

_____

_____

Day Fifteen

"You will grow, you will change"

_____

_____

_____

_____

_____

_____

_____

_____

_____

_____

_____

_____

_____

_____

_____

_____

_____

_____

_____

_____

_____

Day Sixteen

"Let go of who you were"

Day Seventeen

"Become who you were destined to be"

Day Eighteen

"Surround yourself with positive people"

Day Nineteen

"Stay away from <u>Still</u> people, <u>still</u> hating, <u>still</u> complaining"

_____

_____

_____

_____

_____

_____

_____

_____

_____

_____

_____

_____

_____

_____

_____

_____

_____

_____

_____

Day Twenty

"A great future doesn't require a great past"

_____

_____

_____

_____

_____

_____

_____

_____

_____

_____

_____

_____

_____

_____

_____

_____

_____

_____

Day Twenty-One

"Become attentive to your thoughts"

Day Twenty-Two

"A mistake should be your teacher, not your attacker"

Day Twenty-Three

"Don't let anyone stop you from being the best you"

Day Twenty-Four

"Beautiful Minds, Inspire others"

Day Twenty-Five

"You meet people for a blessing or lesson"

Day Twenty-Six

"The secret of change is to focus, on building the new"

_____

_____

_____

_____

_____

_____

_____

_____

_____

_____

_____

_____

_____

_____

_____

_____

_____

_____

_____

_____

Day Twenty-Seven

"Scars are to remind you of the strength after the pain"

_____

_____

_____

_____

_____

_____

_____

_____

_____

_____

_____

_____

_____

_____

_____

_____

_____

_____

_____

Day Twenty-Eight

"God will restore all that you lost"

Day Twenty-Nine

"Believe in your vision, make it happen"

Day Thirty

"A goal without a plan, is just a wish"

Day Thirty-One

"Don't decrease your vision. Increase your efforts"

_____

_____

_____

_____

_____

_____

_____

_____

_____

_____

_____

_____

_____

_____

_____

_____

_____

Day Thirty-Two

"Some dreams are more important than sleep"

Day Thirty-Three

"God is strategically ordering your steps"

_____

_____

_____

_____

_____

_____

_____

_____

_____

_____

_____

_____

_____

_____

_____

_____

_____

_____

Day Thirty-Four

"In a split-second God can resolve any situation"

Section Three

Power of Believing

Inspiration

"Ask, and it will be given to you; seek, and you will find; knock, and it will be opened to you. "For everyone who asks receives, and he who seeks finds, and to him who knocks it will be opened" (Matt. 7:7-8). NKJV

Thought to Ponder:

To ask is to request, or a petition when you ask in prayer you must believe that what you ask will be given to you.

"And whatever things you ask in prayer, believing, you will receive"

(Matt 21:22). NKVJ

There is power in your believing, therefore have faith that what you ask and say with your words will come to pass.

Day Thirty-Five

"The idea comes while we pray"

Day Thirty-Six

"Though I fall, I will rise again"

Day Thirty-Seven

"Nothing will stop God's plan for your life"

Day Thirty-Eight

"Anything is possible when you believe"

Day Thirty-Nine

"God makes a way out of no way"

_____

_____

_____

_____

_____

_____

_____

_____

_____

_____

_____

_____

_____

_____

_____

_____

_____

_____

Day Forty

"God answers when you least expect it, keep praying"

_____

_____

_____

_____

_____

_____

_____

_____

_____

_____

_____

_____

_____

_____

_____

_____

_____

_____

Conclusion

Wow, it is the end of your forty-day journal. How did it feel to spend time with the Father and pour out your thoughts? You stated the declaration at the beginning of this journal. You spoke life, decreed and declared over all areas of your life as you wrote them down. You wrote visions and dreams. And in the last forty-days you POWER Charged your mind with the Power of words. Your words, the affirming quotes, the Empowerment given to you by scripture in the pages of this journal are now positive life for you.

POWER CHARGE Your Mind Empowerment Journal goal was to guide you on a continues path from negative thinking. It is to motivate you in fulfilling positive thoughts, and goals for your life. It is to help you keep your days filled with the presence of God as you speak peace, positive actions, and joy. As the journal pages has ended don't let the pages of into your life end with it. Stay alert to any negative thoughts that try to set shop in your mind.

Remember you have the power to control your thoughts. Instead of criticizing yourself for what's not good enough, pretty or perfect enough on you. Mentally self-check your self and focus on the positive gifts and talents God has given you to share with this world. You are important, beautiful, intelligent, handsome, valuable, and worth the love of yourself.

We are fashioned to think in a different pattern than the negative world. All around you there is negativity and ideas of this world. Now is the time to think on the positive word of God. In doing so we will begin to know what His perfect will is for our lives.

"And do not be conformed to this world, but be ye transformed by the renewing of your mind, that you may prove what is that good and acceptable and perfect will of God"

(Rom. 12:2) NKJV

Congratulations on your new thought process, now walk in the new mind you just recharged and act!

CTA

You can connect with Caris and receive updates on upcoming books at www.carislreed.com. If you are looking for a new path in your life where you can develop in new ideas, or have clarity of your purpose. Caris is a Life Coach, Certified Christian Life Coach. Caris L. Reed The POWer Life Coach LLC you can Schedule a 30-minute free Introductory call on thepowerlifecoach.com.

You can connect with Caris on all her social media platforms:

Instagram:www.instagram.com/carislreed
Facebook: http://fb.me/Godshealinghope
YouTube:https://www.youtube.com/channel/UCzTO8u HIvRtgSJqOlfwal7A?view=
Periscope: http://www.pscp.tv/ThePOWerlifecoach/follow

I'm so excited for you lets us be on one accord lifting the name of Jesus Christ!
Follow, like, share, and subscribe me so together we defeat the enemy in Jesus Christ name Amen

For speaking or event hosting you may contact Caris at info@carislreed.com

"Keep Calm and Trust God"

"The Lord is my light and my salvation who shall I fear"

"I can do all things though Christ who strengthens me"

_____

_____

_____

_____

_____

_____

_____

_____

_____

_____

_____

_____

_____

_____

_____

_____

_____

_____

_____

_____

_____

_____

_____

_____

_____

_____

_____

_____

"This is the day the Lord has made let us rejoice and be glad"

"I will never leave you nor forsake you"

_____

_____

_____

_____

_____

_____

_____

_____

_____

_____

_____

_____

_____

_____

_____

_____

_____

_____

_____

_____

_____

_____

_____

_____

_____

_____

"Be Strong and courageous God is with you"

"The Joy of the Lord is your strength"

Made in the USA
Middletown, DE
04 October 2021